Read for a Better World™

CLOWN FISH

A First Look

PERCY LEED

GRL Consultants,
Diane Craig and Monica Marx,
Certified Literacy Specialists

Lerner Publications ◆ Minneapolis

Educator Toolbox

Reading books is a great way for kids to express what they're interested in. Before reading this title, ask the reader these questions:

What do you think this book is about? Look at the cover for clues.

What do you already know about clown fish?

What do you want to learn about clown fish?

Let's Read Together

Encourage the reader to use the pictures to understand the text.

Point out when the reader successfully sounds out a word.

Praise the reader for recognizing sight words such as *they* and *are*.

TABLE OF CONTENTS

Clown Fish

Clown fish live in warm waters. They swim near coral reefs.

Clown fish
are orange.
They have three
white stripes.

A clown fish is smaller than a teacup.

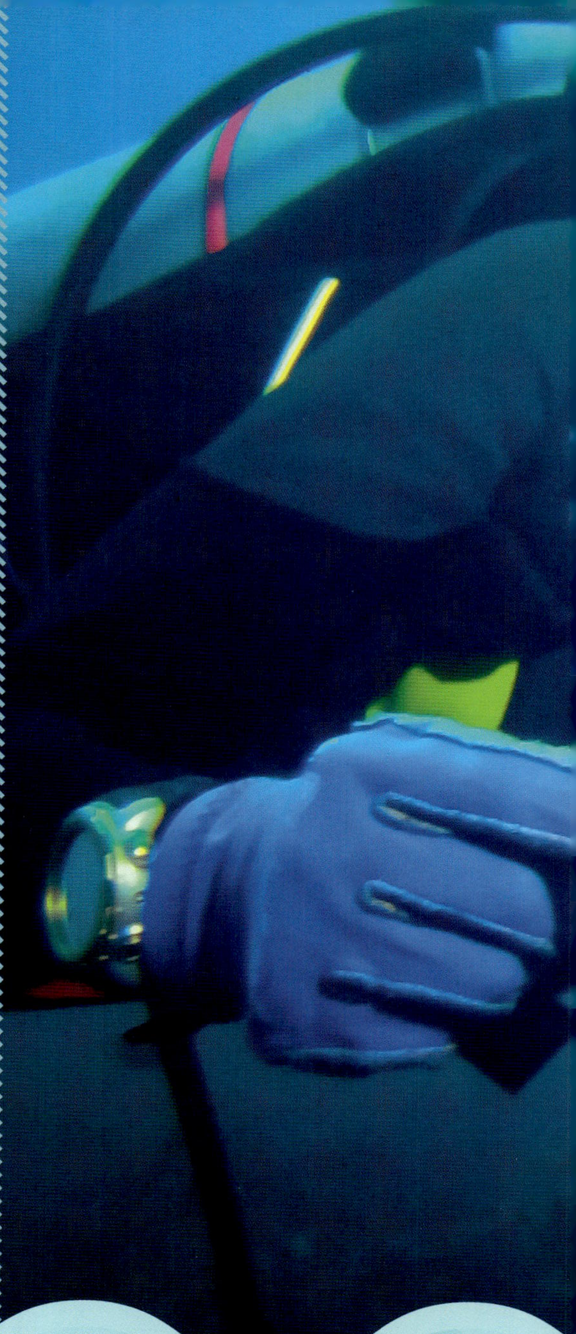

How might
being small be helpful?

Clown fish live in sea anemones.

These are ocean animals.

Sea anemones protect clown fish. Clown fish hide in them.

Clown fish eat algae. They also eat creatures on sea anemones.

How do sea anemones help clown fish?

eggs

Female clown fish
lay eggs.
The males protect
the eggs.

The new clown
fish hatch.
They find sea
anemones to live in.

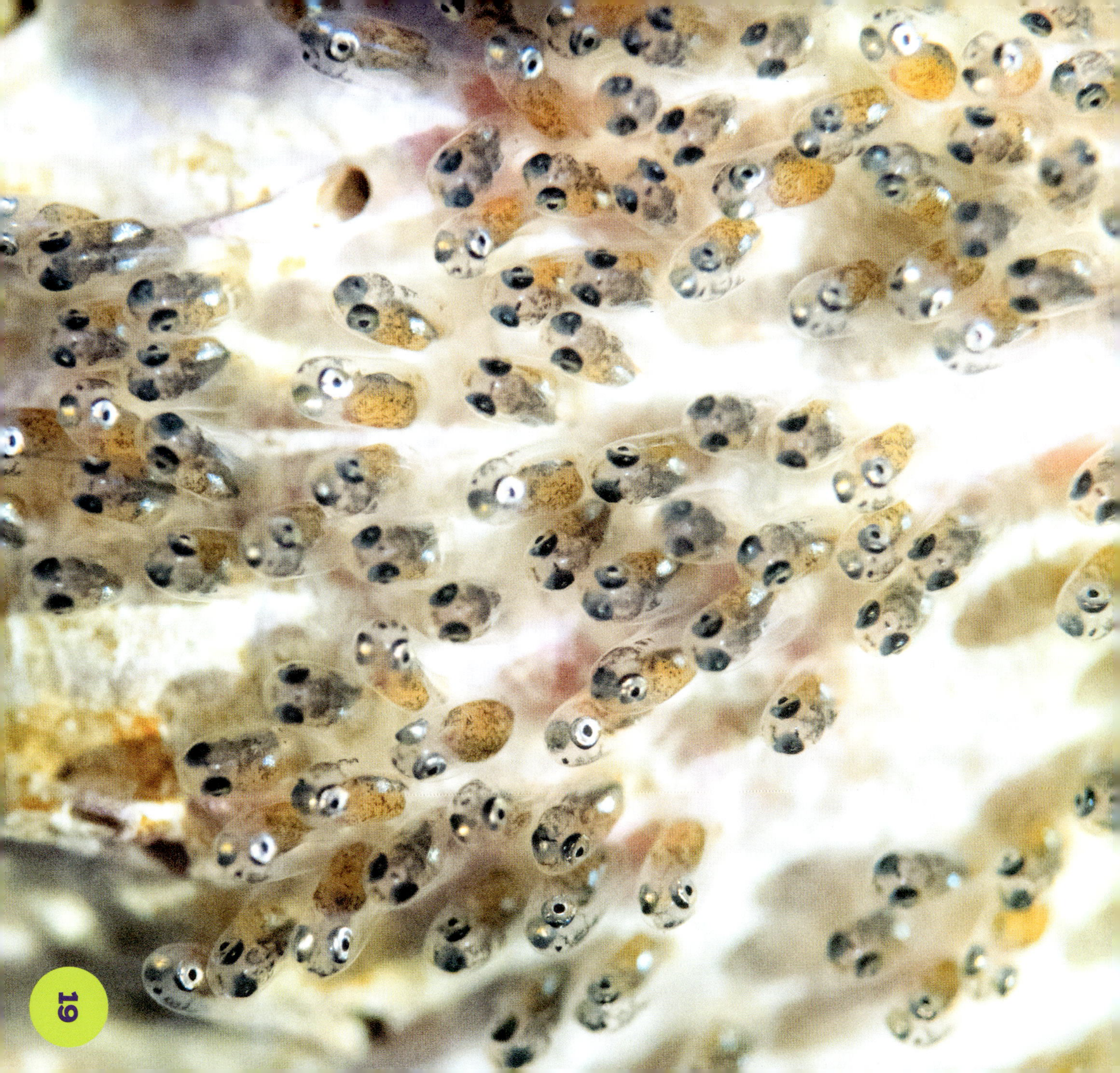

Some clown fish live alone.
Others live in small groups.

You Connect!

What is something you like about clown fish?

Have you ever seen a fish in a lake, ocean, or pond?

What other ocean animals do you know about?

STEM Snapshot

Encourage students to think and ask questions like scientists. Ask the reader:

What is something you learned about clown fish?

What is something you noticed about sea anemones?

What is something you still want to learn about clown fish?

Photo Glossary

coral reef

eggs

sea anemone

stripes

Learn More

Peters, Katie. *I See the Ocean*. Minneapolis: Lerner Publications, 2020.

Schuetz, Kari. *Clownfish and Sea Anemones*. Minneapolis: Bellwether Media, 2019.

Vink, Amanda. *Sea Anemones Are Brainless!* New York: Gareth Stevens, 2020.

Index

Photo Acknowledgments

The images in this book are used with the permission of: © FGorgun/iStockphoto, pp. 6–7, 23 (stripes); © Jack PhotoWarp/Shutterstock Images, pp. 8–9; © joebelanger/iStockphoto, p. 17 (eggs); © John A. Anderson/Shutterstock Images, p. 11; © JoyfulThailand/iStockphoto, pp. 16–17, 23 (eggs); © lindsay_imagery/iStockphoto, pp. 12–13; © LuffyKun/iStockphoto, p. 20; © manpuku7/iStockphoto, pp. 14–15; © marrio31/iStockphoto, pp. 18–19; © Mumemories/iStockphoto, pp. 4–5, 23 (coral reef); © VM_Studio/iStockphoto, pp. 10, 23 (sea anemone).

Cover Photo: © Artur Arantes Fh/Shutterstock Images

Design Elements: Mighty Media, Inc.

Lerner Publications Company
An imprint of Lerner Publishing Group, Inc.
241 First Avenue North
Minneapolis, MN 55401 USA

For reading levels and more information, look up this title at www.lernerbooks.com.

Main body text set in Mikado a Medium.
Typeface provided by Hannes von Doehren.

Library of Congress Cataloging-in-Publication Data

Names: Leed, Percy, 1968- author.
Title: Clown fish : a first look / Percy Leed.
Description: Minneapolis : Lerner Publications, [2023] | Series: Read about ocean animals (read for a better world) | Audience: Ages 5–8 | Audience: Grades K–1 | Summary: "Clown fish are iconic creatures of coral reefs. Simple text and engaging photos introduce readers to these colorful ocean animals"– Provided by publisher.
Identifiers: LCCN 2021040257 (print) | LCCN 2021040258 (ebook) | ISBN 9781728459103 (library binding) | ISBN 9781728461694 (ebook)
Subjects: LCSH: Anemonefishes—Juvenile literature. | Coral reef fishes—Juvenile literature.
Classification: LCC QL638.P77 L44 2023 (print) | LCC QL638.P77 (ebook) | DDC 597/.72—dc23

LC record available at https://lccn.loc.gov/2021040257
LC ebook record available at https://lccn.loc.gov/2021040258

Manufactured in the United States of America
1 - CG - 7/15/22